Samsung Galaxy A35 5G User Manual For Seniors

A Detailed Step by Step Manual For First Time Setup, Configuration and Usage That Includes Tips, Tricks and Screenshots

Jazz K. Famous

Table of Contents

Introduction 14

Chapter One 16

Turn on device 17

Use the setup wizard 18

Transfer data from old device 18

Lock or unlock your device 19

    Side button settings 19

    Press twice 20

    Press and hold 20

Account 21

    Add Google account 21

    Add Samsung account 21

    Add Outlook account 22

Set up voicemail 22

Navigation 23

Navigation Bar 26

    Navigation key 27

    Navigation gestures 27

Customize home screen 28

    Application icon 28

    Wallpaper 29

    Themes 30

    Icon 30

Widget 31

Custom widgets 31

Home screen settings 32

Simple mode 35

Status Bar 37

Notification panel 38

View the notification panel 38

Quick settings 39

Quick settings options 40

Bixby 41

The Vision of Bixby 41

Camera 41

Gallery 41

Internet 42

Patterns and routines 42

Digital wellbeing and Parental Controls 43

Always On Display 45

AOD theme 46

Chapter Two 47

Biometric security 47

Face recognition 47

Face recognition management 48

Fingerprint scanner 49

Fingerprint management 49

Fingerprint verification settings 50

Biometric settings 51

Multiple windows 51

Window control 53

Edge panel...54

Apps panel 54

Configure edge panel..56

Edge panel position and style 57

About the edge panel 58

Enter text 58

Toolbar 59

Configure Samsung keyboard 62

Chapter Three 66

Camera and Gallery 66

Camera..66

Navigate camera screen..67

Configure recording mode 68

AR Zone...71

Record video 72

Camera settings 72

Gallery..77

View pictures 77

Edit photos..79

Play video..80

Edit video 81

Share videos and photos 82

Delete videos and photos 82

Group similar images together 83

Screenshot 83

Palm slide screenshot 83

Screenshot settings 84

Screen recorder... 85

Screen recorder settings 86

Chapter Four 87

Applications.. 87

Disable or uninstall an application 87

Search application.. 87

Sort applications 88

Create and use folders 88

Copy folders to any home screen.. 89

Delete any folder... 89

Game booster.. 90

Application settings... 91

Calendar 92

Add calendar 92

Calendar reminder style.. 93

Generate event 94

Delete event.. 94

Chapter Five 95

Contact 95

    Create contact 95

    Edit contact 96

    Favorites 96

    Share contacts 97

    View contacts when sharing content 97

Groups 98

    Create a group 98

    Delete or add group contact 99

    Send message to group 99

    Send email to group 100

    Delete group 100

    Merge contacts 101

    Import contacts 102

    Export contacts 102

    Mobile contacts 102

    Sync contacts 103

    Delete contact 103

    Emergency contact 103

Internet 105

    Browser tabs 105

    Create bookmark 106

    Open bookmark 106

Save page 106

View history 107

Share page.. 107

Secret mode 108

Secret mode settings..................................... 108

Turn off secret mode.................................... 109

Internet settings 109

Message 110

Message search... 110

Delete conversation 111

Emergency messaging................................... 111

Message settings... 112

Emergency alerts... 112

My File.. 114

File groups 114

My File settings 115

Telephone... 117

Phone call.. 117

Make a call 118

Make a call using Recent Calls..................... 118

Using your Contacts to make calls 118

Answer a call 119

Reject a call 119

Reject call and leave a message 120

End call 120

Actions during a telephone conversation 120

Switch to speaker or headphones...........................120

Multitasking 121

Call background 121

Incoming call pop-up settings 122

Manage calls 123

Call log...123

Save contacts from recent calls 123

Delete call record 124

Block a number 124

Speed Dial 125

Make a call using speed dial 126

Delete speed dial number................................126

Emergency calls..126

Phone settings..127

Optional calling services 127

Call multiple participants 128

Video call..128

Video call effect...129

Wireless calling 129

Real Time Text (RTT)..130

Samsung Health 132

Before beginning a workout..................................132

Samsung Notes 134

    Create a note 135

    Voice recording 135

    Edit notes 135

    Note option 136

    Notes menu 137

Chapter Six 138

Access Settings 138

    Search settings 138

Connections 139

    Wi-Fi 139

    Connect to a hidden Wi-Fi network 139

    Intelligent Wi-Fi settings 141

    Advanced Wi-Fi settings 142

    Direct Wi-Fi 143

    Disconnect Wi-Fi Direct 144

Bluetooth 144

    Rename paired device 145

    Unpairing a Bluetooth device 146

    Advanced Bluetooth settings 146

    Dual audio 148

Near Field Communication (NFC) and Payments 148

    Click and pay 149

Airplane 149

Mobile network 150

Mobile hotspot 152

Set mobile hotspot settings 153

Auto hotspot 154

Tethering 154

Ethernet 155

Unblock the network 155

Connect devices 156

Sound and vibration 158

Sound mode 158

Mute with gesture 159

Vibration 159

Volume 161

Using the media volume buttons 162

Media volume limit 162

Ringtone 163

Notification sound 163

Notification 164

App notification 164

Lock screen notification 164

Notification popup style 165

Do not disturb 166

Advanced notification settings 168

Notifications when picking up the smartphone 170

11

Display 170

    Dark mode 170

    Screen brightness 171

    Motion smoothness 172

    Eye comfort shield 172

    Screen mode 173

    Font size and font style 173

    Screen zoom 174

    Full screen application 174

    Camera crop 175

    Screen timeout 175

    Prevent accidental contact 176

    Touch sensitivity 176

    Display charging information 176

    Screen saver 177

    Lift up and wake up 177

    Double click to open screen 178

    Double tap to turn off screen 178

    The screen stays on while watching 178

    One handed mode 179

Lock screen and security 179

    Screen lock type 180

    Set up a secure screen lock 180

Chapter Seven 183

Troubleshooting 183

    Software updates or system updates............183

Reset to default...185

    Reset all settings 185

    Reset network settings.................................185

    Reset accessibility settings..........................186

    Restore factory data....................................186

Introduction

Samsung Galaxy A35 User Guide Introduction
Modern smartphones like the Samsung Galaxy A35 are made to be simple to use and seamless for consumers. It's crucial to know how to use and maximize your Phone given its amazing features and capabilities. This user guide covers a wide range of topics, including [1]: giving you a thorough overview of the Samsung Galaxy A35.

- **Activation and Setup**: Discover how to transfer files from your old device and set up your new one, as well as how to activate and set up your Samsung Galaxy A35.

- *Device Tutorial*: Learn how to use your Samsung Galaxy A35 with interactive instructions, along with helpful hints to improve your experience.
- *Top Features and Functions*: Learn how to make use of key features like notification management, screen lock, and camera settings.
- *Troubleshooting*: Discover fixes for typical difficulties, such restarting your gadget, clearing the preferences for apps, and fixing connectivity issues.
- *Tips & Tricks*: Make the most of your Samsung Galaxy A35 by following professional tips on productivity, customization, and other topics.

Device layout and functions

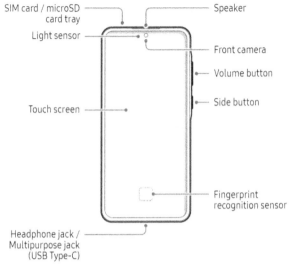

SIM card / microSD card tray
Light sensor
Touch screen
Headphone jack / Multipurpose jack (USB Type-C)

Speaker
Front camera
Volume button
Side button
Fingerprint recognition sensor

Microphone
Rear camera
Flash
Speaker
Air vent hole

GPS antenna
NFC antenna
Main antenna
Microphone

Chapter One
Turn on device

Press the side button to power up your gadget. Do not use the gadget if it has any cracks or breaks in the body. As soon as the device is fixed, put it to use.

○ Press and hold the side button to activate the gadget.

• You can power down your device by holding down the Side and Volume keys at the same time. Press to give your approval when asked.

• Press and hold the Side and Volume keys at the same time, then press Restart, to restart the device. Then, when asked, provide your approval.

Note: A very strong 5G connection and unobstructed antennas (on the back of the device) are required for excellent 5G performance. To find out if the network is available, contact the service providers. Keep in mind that a cover or case can reduce 5G performance.

Use the setup wizard

Setup Wizard walks you through the basics of customizing your device the first time you switch it on.

Just follow the on-screen instructions to set your preferred language, connect to a Wi-Fi network, set up your accounts, choose location services, learn about your device's capabilities, and much more.

Transfer data from old device

The Smart Switch can be downloaded to help you move media files, contacts, calendar events, notes, images, videos, messages, and more from your old smartphone to your new one. With a USB cable, computer, or Wi-Fi, the Smart Switch can transfer your data.

1. Navigate to Accounts & backup in the Settings menu, and then select Bring info from the old device.

2. After you see the prompts, select the files you want to transfer.

Lock or unlock your device

Protect your device by using the screen lock feature. Your smartphone will lock itself when the screen times out by default.

Side key/Fingerprint scanner
Press to lock.
Press to turn on the screen, and then swipe the screen to unlock it.

Side button settings

It is possible to change the default shortcuts for the Side key.

Press twice

You can choose which functions are activated when the Side button is pressed twice.

1. To access the side key, go to the Settings menu, then touch Advanced features.
2. To activate this function, touch the double push button. Then, touch the options:
*   Cameras with a quick launch (the default)
*   Launch applications

Press and hold

Pick which features will be activated when you press and hold the side key.

1. Select Advanced Features from the Settings menu, and then press the Side key.
2. Find the following choices under the "Press & hold" heading:
*   The default is Wake Bixby.
*   Menus for turning off the power.

Account

Get the accounts set up and running.

Note: Some accounts may have functionality for things like calendars, contacts, and email.

Add Google account

To use Google Cloud Storage, apps installed directly from the account, and all of Android features, log in to your Google Account.

You may activate Google Devices Protection by logging into your Google Account and then setting the lock screen. For factory resets, this service requires data from your Google Account.

1. Navigate directly to Manage accounts from the Settings menu by touching Accounts & backup.

2. Select "Add account" and then "Google."

Add Samsung account

To get full access to Samsung content and utilize all of Samsung's apps, you need to log in to your Samsung account.

o   Go to the Settings menu and then tap on Your Account.

Add Outlook account

To access and organize your email messages, log in to your Outlook account.

1. Navigate directly to Manage accounts from the Settings menu by touching 🔄 Accounts & backup.

2. After that, choose Outlook from the list of accounts.

Set up voicemail

When you initially use the voicemail service, you have the option to configure it. The Phone app allows you to access your voicemail.

1. To access voicemail on your phone, press and hold the 🔢 1 key or tap 📧 Voicemail.

2. To create a password, record a greeting, and add your own name, just follow the instructions.

Navigation

The capacitive stylus or your finger's pad provides the lightest touch that a touch screen can respond to. The surface of the screen could be damaged if you use too much force or if you place metallic objects on it; the warranty will not cover this.

Touch

To choose or open an object, you should use a light touch.

- A simple touch of an item will choose it.
- You can zoom in or out of a picture by double-tapping on it.

Swipe

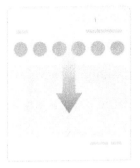

To drag your finger across your screen, do so lightly.

- To open your phone, just swipe the screen.

- The Home screen and menu items can be accessed by swiping your screen.

Drag and drop

Move an object by tapping and holding it and dragging it to a new location.

- To quickly add an app shortcut to the Home screen, just drag it.

- You can move a widget around by dragging it to a new spot.

Zoom in and out

To zoom in and out, use your index finger and thumb either together or independently on the screen.

- To easily zoom in, spread your fingers apart on the screen.
- To easily zoom out, press and hold your thumb and forefinger on the screen.

Touch and hold

Items can be activated by touching and holding them.

- To access the settings menu, touch and hold the field.

- The Home screen may be customized by touching and holding it.

Navigation Bar

Either the navigation keys or full screen gestures can be used to navigate your device.

Recent apps ———————————————— Back

Home

Navigation key

To quickly move about, use the arrow keys that run along the bottom of your screen.

1. To access the buttons, go to the Display section of Settings, then press Navigation bar.
2. Select the side of your screen where you want the Back and Recent apps icons to appear by tapping the option beneath the Button order.

Navigation gestures

To avoid any distractions when using your screen, hide the navigation buttons at the bottom of the screen. To navigate the gadget, just swipe instead.

1. To enable the feature, go to Settings > Display > Navigation bar > Swipe gesture.
2. Customize with the touch of a button:

- More: Select Gesture type & sensitivity.
- Point out the locations of all the screen gestures by displaying lines at the bottom of the screen.
- You can still use the gesture to switch between programs even after you've deactivated the

gesture suggestion, provided you've enabled this option.

- If your device is in portrait mode, you can hide the keyboard by showing the symbol in the bottom right corner of your screen.

Customize home screen

The device's home screen is where you'll want to begin your navigational journey. Here you may arrange your preferred apps and widgets, create additional Home screens, hide screens, rearrange their order, and choose the main Home screen.

Application icon

You can access your apps from any of the Home screens by using their icons.

o Choose an app from the Applications menu, hold down its icon, and then tap the ⊞ Add to Home button.

To delete the icon:

o Launch an app from the Home screen, then press and hold its icon and click 🗑 to remove it.

Note: Deleting an icon from the Home screen does not remove the icon from the program itself.

Wallpaper

You can personalize the look of your device's Lock and Home screens by choosing a wallpaper, movie, or picture from your gallery.

1. Press and hold the Home screen until you see ⊡ Wallpaper & style.

2. Select a wallpaper from the options by tapping on one of the menus below:

- Edit the images on the Home screen and the Lock screen with a touch.

- You can change the wallpaper by choosing one of several alternatives or by downloading more from the Galaxy Themes.

- Color palette: Pick a color scheme that complements the wallpaper you already have.

- Turn on Dark mode to apply it to the wallpaper: Toggle on Dark mode to apply it to the wallpaper.

Themes

Set the background, app icons, Lock screen, and Home screen themes to your liking.

1. Press and hold the screen on the Home screen.

2. You may preview and download themes by pressing the 🖌 Themes button.

3. To access downloaded themes, go to ☰ Menu > Tap My things > Themes.

4. To apply a theme, touch on it and then press Apply.

Icon

The default icons can be replaced by applying different sets of icons.

1. Press and hold the screen when on the Home screen.

2. To preview and download it, click 🖌 Themes > Icons and tap on icon set.

3. To see the icons you've downloaded, click ☰ Menu, touch My things, and then press Icons.

4. To apply your chosen icon set, touch an icon and then press Apply.

Widget

You can add widgets to your home screen to make it easier to access specific information or apps.

1. Press and hold the screen on the Home screen.

2. To access the widget sets, go to ⬚◇ Widgets and tap on them.

3. Just find the widget you want to add to your home screen and touch the Add button.

Custom widgets

After you've added a widget, you can change its position and behavior as you like.

o Press and hold a widget on the Home screen until an option appears:

• ⊞ : To create a stack, simply add more widgets of the same size to the same location on the screen.

• 🗑 Deleting: Eliminates the widget from the display.

- ⚙ Settings: Modifies the widgets' look and behavior.

- ⓘ : Review the widget's usage, permissions, and more in the app's details.

Home screen settings

Customize the screens for Home and Applications.

1. Press and hold the screen on the Home screen.

2. To proceed with customization, touch ⚙ Settings:

- Home screen layout: You can configure the device to have separate Home and Applications screens, or you can only have the Home screen with all the apps.

- The grid for home screens: alter the arrangement of icons on your home screen by selecting from available layouts.

- To change the icon arrangement in the Applications panel, go to the grid and choose a layout.

- Folder Grid: To change the arrangement of folders.

- Sliding to the right from your Home screens to see the media page when enabled adds media pages to Home screens. Press to access media services that are accessible.

- Make the Applications screen easily accessible from home screens: Include a button on your home screens to bring up our applications screen.

- Prevents the removal or repositioning of objects from your Home screens by locking their arrangement.

- You can set it so that any apps you download will be automatically added to your Home screen.

- To hide apps from the Home and Applications screens, you can select which ones to hide. Return to this screen in order to retrieve concealed apps. Even after you hide an app from Finder, it may still be installed and appear in search results.

- To show badges on apps that have current notifications, activate the feature. Badge styles can be chosen as well.

- If you want to access the notification pane from any location on your home screen, you can activate the "Swipe downward for notification pane" option.

- Switching to landscape mode: When you go from portrait to landscape mode, your Home screen will automatically rotate.

- View version details in the "About" section of the home screen.

- Give us a call: Contact Samsung's support team through Samsung's Member portal.

Simple mode

The layout in Easy mode is more casual because the icons and text are larger. You can switch between your default screen layout and a somewhat more basic one.

Recent apps — Back

Home

1. Select Easy mode from the Display menu in the settings.

2. To enable this function, simply touch . The following choices will show up:

- To set the delay before continuous touches are recognized as touch and hold, go to the "Touch & hold delay" section.

- Choose a keyboard with colors that stand out from the rest.

Status Bar

On the right side, you can see device information, and on the left, you can see notification alerts.

Status symbol

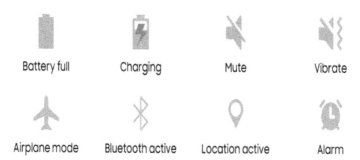

| Battery full | Charging | Mute | Vibrate |

| Airplane mode | Bluetooth active | Location active | Alarm |

Notification icon

| Missed calls | Call in progress | New message | Voicemail |

| New email | Download | Upload | App update |

Customize the status bar's display settings with ease.

Tip: To customize the notifications that appear in the Status bar, go to the Quick settings, press More options, and finally select Status bar.

Notification panel

Just open your Notification panel to quickly access settings, notifications, and more.

View the notification panel

From any of the screens, you can reach the Notification pane.

1. The Notification pane can be accessed by swiping down on the screen.

- Touching an object will open it.

- You can remove a single notice by dragging it to the right or left.

- Press Clear to dismiss all alerts.

- To personalize your notifications, go to the settings and tap on Notifications.

2. To quickly dismiss the notification panel, either touch the ‹Back button or drag it up from the bottom of your screen.

Quick settings

The device's functionalities can be quickly accessed through the notification pane by employing Quick settings. The most common settings on Quick settings are shown by the icons below. Activation and deactivation cause the icon colors to change. It is possible that your device has additional settings.

1. Use the scroll bar to bring up the notification window.

2. To access Quick settings, swipe down from the top of the screen once more.

- Toggle it's on/off status with the touch of a button.

- Press and hold the icon for the quick setting to access the setting.

Quick settings options

The following settings can be accessed using the Quick settings menu.

- Finders: Look through your gadget.

- Power-off: ability to power off and restart.

- Settings: Quickly access the device's menu for configuring it.

- Additional choices: rearrange quick settings and change the layout of buttons.

- The Device Control: When compatible apps like SmartThings or Google Home are installed, you can manage other devices.

- Media outputs: open the Media pane and manage the playback of any audio or video devices that are attached.

- Slider for screen brightness: drag to adjust.

Bixby

This virtual assistant changes, learns, and adjusts based on the user's preferences. In addition to learning your habits, it integrates with the apps you use most and lets you customize your reminders based on time and place.

- o On the Home screen, press and hold the Side key.

The Vision of Bixby

To help you make sense of what you see, this Bixby integrates with your Gallery, Camera, and Internet apps. You can use the contextual icons for things like translations, QR code scanning, landmark identification, and purchasing.

Camera

You can use Bixby's Vision to better interpret what you see through the camera's viewfinder.

- o Touch More > then Bixby Vision and follow the on-screen instructions from the Camera.

Gallery

You can use the Bixby Vision in photos and images saved in the Gallery app.

1. Select a photo to see it in the ✳ Gallery by touching it.

2. Engage 👁 Bixby Vision by touching the screen and following the on-screen instructions.

Internet

When you look at a picture on the web, the Bixby Vision can tell you more about it.

1. While browsing the web, press and hold a picture until a menu appears.

2. Get directions by touching the screen and utilizing Bixby Vision.

Patterns and routines

You may program your smartphone to adapt its settings to different activities and situations with the help of modes and routines.

o Select ✓ Modes & Routines from the Settings menu for the following pages:

• Pick a mode that suits your current activity or location.

- Routines: Set up scheduled actions for your phone based on when or where you are.

Digital wellbeing and Parental Controls

If you want a simple way to manage and monitor your digital habits, you can obtain daily views of your app usage, alert volume, and device check rates. You may program your device to help you relax even in the hours leading up to bedtime.

  o To access the options listed below, go to Settings and then tap Digital Wellbeing & parental control:

- Access the following by tapping the Dashboard:

- Check the daily launch and usage duration of the app with the screens time feature.

- Notifications received: You may see the total number of app notifications each day.

- View the daily total of app launches or unlocks in the "Times launched" section.

- Set a daily average and customise your screens time target in the Settings app.

- You can limit the amount of time you spend using each program each day with application timers.

- While driving, you can use the screen time while linked to your car's Bluetooth to keep tabs on the apps you use most often.

- Volume monitor: Choose the sound source to monitor the volume and shield your hearing from potential loud noises.

- Google's Families Link program allows parents to keep tabs on their children's online activities. It was possible to select apps, filter contents, keep track of screen time, and establish screen time limitations.

Always On Display

Use Always-On-Display (AOD) to view the time, date, and any notifications (such as missed calls or messages) without unlocking the smartphone.

1. Select Always-On-Display from the 🔒 Lock screen menu in Settings.

2. Select the following options after touching to activate the feature:

- If you want to see a clock and notifications even while your phone isn't in use, you can adjust that setting.

- You may customize the look of your lock screen and always-on display clock by adjusting its design and color settings.

- When using FaceWidgets' music controls, you can see the current track name, artist, and album information shown.

- Choose between landscape and portrait modes to display AOD on your screen.

- Auto-brightness: set the Always-On-Display to automatically adjust the brightness.

- Use the Always-On-Display to see the current software version and license details.

AOD theme

For Always-On-Display, use a custom theme.

1. Press and hold the Home screen to access the 🖌 Themes, and then tap on the AODs.

- Simply touching an AOD will bring up a preview and allow you to download it to your My Always-On-Displays.

2. To access the themes you've downloaded, go to ☰ Menu > My things > AODs.

3. Press Apply after touching an AOD.

Chapter Two
Biometric security

Enable biometrics for secure device unlocking and account login.

Face recognition

Turning this on will unlock the screen. A PIN, pattern, or password can be set up so that you can use your face to unlock the device.

- A pattern, password, or PIN is more secure than facial recognition. You never know who could be able to open your device just by looking like you.

- Wearing a hat, glasses, beard, or a lot of makeup can mess with face recognition.

- Be sure your camera lens is clean and that you're in a well-lit area before you register your face.

1. To enable face recognition, go to the Settings menu, and then touch on Security & privacy. From there, choose Biometrics.

47

2. Follow the on-screen instructions to register your face.

Face recognition management

Make adjustments to how face recognition works.

- o To access the face recognition feature, go to the Settings menu, then touch 🔵 Security & privacy. From there, press Biometrics.

- Remove existing faces: Delete face data.

- Change your appearance to boost recognition: Change your appearance to boost facial recognition.

- You can activate or deactivate the security of facial recognition with the face unlock feature.

- If your device unlocks with a face recognition system, you'll need to remain in the lock screen until you swipe to unlock.

- You can only use facial recognition if your eyes are open, so keep that in mind.

- If you want to make sure that the face can be seen in low light, you can temporarily raise the screen's brightness.

- Facial recognition: Find out how to secure your device with this innovative technology.

Fingerprint scanner

Instead of entering passwords by hand, use fingerprint recognition for certain apps.

When logging into your Samsung account, you can now use your fingerprint as an additional form of authentication. You must configure a PIN, password, or pattern before you may utilize your fingerprints as an unlock method.

1. To access fingerprints, go to Settings > ⬤ Security & privacy > Biometrics.

2. To register your fingerprint, just follow the on-screen instructions.

Fingerprint management

The ability to add, removes, and rename fingerprints.

○ To access the following options, go to Settings > ⬤ Security & privacy > Biometrics > Fingerprints:

49

- The fingerprint registration list is located at the top of the list. To change its name or delete it, just tap on the fingerprint.

- Add fingerprints: To register a new fingerprint, just follow the on-screen instructions.

- Scan the fingerprint to check if it has been registered. This will verify the added fingerprint.

Fingerprint verification settings

Make use of fingerprint recognition to verify your identity in compatible apps and when performing certain actions.

○ To access fingerprints, go to the Settings menu, then tap ⬤ Security & privacy. From there, tap Biometrics.

- Fingerprint unlock: Unlock your device with the touch of a finger.

- You can scan fingerprints even when the screen is off because the fingerprint feature is always active.

- When you power down your device, the screen will display your fingerprint icon.

- If you're utilizing fingerprint verification, you can make the unlock animation appear.

- Fingerprints: Acquire further knowledge regarding the use of fingerprints for device security.

Biometric settings

Make your biometric security preferences known.

o To access biometrics, go to Settings > Security & privacy > Biometrics.

- Effects of display unlock transitions: When you use biometrics to just unlock your device, you'll see effects of display transitions.

- More information regarding biometric security for unlocking your device is available here.

Multiple windows

Use a number of programs simultaneously to do a number of tasks. You can use the split screen to run many applications at once if they allow multi-window. You may resize the windows of your applications and switch between them easily.

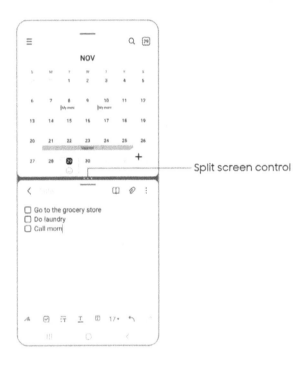

Split screen control

1. Select ||| Recent Apps from the screen.

2. To open the app in split screen mode, tap its icon and then touch Open.

3. To add an app to the split-screen view, touch it in one of the other windows.

- To resize the window, simply drag the middle of its border.

Window control

The way program windows are shown in split screens view can be adjusted using these Window settings.

1. For window resizing, drag the middle of the window's border.

2. Pressing the middle of the window's edge will bring up the following choices:

- ↑↓Window Swap: Rearrange the two windows.

- Add app pair: You may create and add an application pair shortcut to your home screen or applications edge panel by following these steps.

Edge panel

You may access the various customizable panels on these by merely dragging them from the screen's edge. In addition to watching sports, news, and other information, the Edge panels could be used to access tasks, apps, and contacts.

- o You may activate this function by going to Settings, then touching 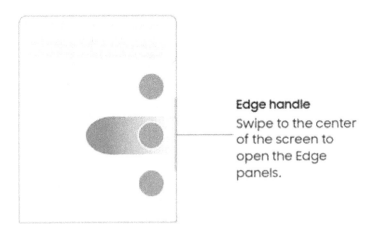 Display. Then, locate the Edge panels and touch.

Edge handle
Swipe to the center of the screen to open the Edge panels.

Apps panel

Inside the Applications window, you can insert new applications.

54

1. To move the Edge handle to the screen's center, you can do so from any screen. To access the Applications pane, swipe left or right.

2. Pressing on a shortcut for an app or app pair will open it. To see all of the apps, you may also tap ⋮⋮⋮ All applications.

• By dragging the program icon from the Applications pane to your open screen, you can launch multiple windows on pop-up views.

The panel for configuring applications:

1. Move the Edge handle to the screen's center from anywhere on it. To access the Applications pane, swipe left or right.

2. Press the ✎ Edit button to add more apps to the Applications window.

• Drag and drop an app from the left side of your screen into an available spot on the right column to add it to the Applications window.

- To create a shortcut for a folder, just drag the program from the left side of the screen to the right column of the screen.

- In order to rearrange the apps on the panel, simply drag and drop them to the desired spot.

- Push the Remove button to uninstall an app.

3. Access your saved modifications by touching the ⟨ "Back" button.

Configure edge panel

You can personalize the edge panels.

1. Press ⚙ Display in the Settings menu, then tap Edge panels, and finally Panels.

2. Here are the available options:

- ✅ The checkbox: turn on or off each window

- Create distinct panels in the editor (if one is available).

- 🔍 : Look for panels that are either already installed or can be easily installed.

- ⋮ More:

- You can rearrange the panels by dragging them to the right or left.

- Uninstall: Get rid of any Edge window that you may have downloaded to your device.

- Select panels to hide on the lock screen in the event that a safe screen lock is enabled.

• Browse the Galaxy Store for more Edge panels and download them right to your device.

3. Access your saved modifications by touching the ‹ "Back" button.

Edge panel position and style

The Edge handle's position is adjustable.

○ Navigate to the following options in the Settings menu: Display > Edge panels > Then Handle:

• ⌄ : You can move the Edge handles along the screen's edge by dragging them.

• Position: Choose Left or Right to set the side on which the Edge displays appear.

- To prevent the location of your handle from being moved merely by touching and holding it, activate the lock feature.

- Style: Choose a hue for the sides of the Edge container.

- Transparency: Adjust the visibility of your Edge handle by dragging the slider.

- The size of the Edge handle can be adjusted by dragging the slider.

- Width: Adjust the width of the Edge handle by dragging the slider.

About the edge panel

The current software version and license information for the Edge panels' feature can be viewed.

- ○ To get information about the Edge panels, go to the ⚙ Display section of the Settings menu, then hit Edge panels.

Enter text

Use either your voice or the keyboard to enter text.

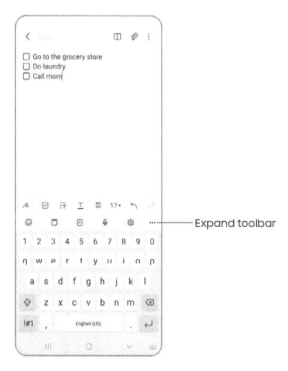

Expand toolbar

Toolbar

This way, you can quickly access all of your keyboard's functions. The service providers differ in their options.

- o To access the following settings from your Samsung keyboard, press the ••• "Expand toolbars" button:

- • ⊙ : Explore different types of GIFs and emojis, create your own unique combination emojis, and much more in the Expression section.

- ⊟ Copy and Paste: Obtain the contents of your clipboard.

- ⊟ Keyboards designed for usage with one hand: Change to that layout.

- 🎤 : Utilize Samsung's voice input feature.

- ⊞ : For example, you can use split keyboards by switching to the separated version of the keyboard.

- ⌨ : One option is to switch to a floating keyboard, which you can then drag and drop to any part of the screen.

- ⚙ Settings: Get to the keyboard's preferences.

- 🔍 : Find particular words or phrases in discussions using the search function.

- : You can use the "Translate" feature to convert text from one language to another simply by typing in a phrase or word.

- Text extraction: identify the content you want to use and then pull out the relevant texts.

- : Use biometrics with the Samsung Pass for quick and secure access to your personal information and online accounts.

- : Get Grammarly's suggestions while you type with this useful tool.

- : Include an emoji in your message.

- GIFs: Feel free to incorporate animated GIFs.

- : Create your own emoji with Bitmoji and use it in the stickers.

- Mojitok: Customize stickers or find ones suggested by the app.

61

- Create your own emoji and use it in the stickers with the augmented reality feature.

- Keyboard dimensions: Change the keyboard's width and height.

- Text editing: With the help of an editing pane, you may highlight the text you want to copy, cut, and paste.

Configure Samsung keyboard

Personalize your Samsung keyboard with your own choices.

○ Press Settings for the following options on the Samsung keyboard:

- Languages and types: Select the languages that you want to be able to type on your keyboard and set the keyboard type.

- Just swipe the Space bar to the right or left to change languages.

Smart typing

- Auto-suggestive texts: see suggested expressions and words as you type.

- To spice up your predictive text, try adding some emoticons.

- You can see stickers that the app thinks you might like while you type.

- Auto-replace: The suggestions made by the predictive texts will automatically replace anything you typed.

- Suggest textual edits by highlighting red the incorrect words and offering suggestions for their repairs.

- Shortcuts in text: make short cuts for the terms you use most.

- Additional input options: Personalize additional typing choices.

Arrangement & style

- Keyboard toolbars: You can choose to show or hide them.

- You may make the keys stand out more against the background by adjusting the size and color of your Samsung keyboard. This is known as a high contrast keyboard.

- Theme: Select a theme for the keyboard.

- Mode: Choose between portrait and landscape orientation.

- Toggle the keyboard's size and transparency.

- Layout: Make your keyboard's numbers and special characters visible.

- You can alter the text size by dragging the slider.

- Make changes to the keyboard shortcuts for custom symbols.

Additional Configurations

The first step is to set up the voice input services and preferences.

- Customize the gestures and feedback for touch, swipe, and more.

- Enable the feature to copy and paste screenshots to the clipboard.

- Select content from outside sources to use: Enable the functions of the third-party keyboard.

- Return the keyboard to its factory settings and erase all user data by resetting to the defaults.

Chapter Three
Camera and Gallery

With the Camera app, you can take stunning photos and videos. You may see and edit the videos and photographs that you store in the Gallery.

Camera

Take advantage of all the features and options available in the professional lens and video editing suite.

- Choose  "Camera" from the list of apps.

TIP: Just press the Side key twice fast to open the camera app.

Settings

Zoom

Shooting modes

Gallery

Switch cameras

Capture

Navigate camera screen

Take breathtaking images using your device's front
and back cameras.

1. To set up your shot, go to Camera and then
   use the options below:

- Press and hold the screen where you want the
  camera to concentrate.

- The screen's brightness scale will become visible upon screen touch. To adjust the brightness, simply drag the slider.

• Swiping up or down the screen quickly toggles between the front and back cameras.

• To focus on a given level of zoom, press an option at the bottom of the screen and then touch 1x. (Enabled exclusively when using the back camera.)

• Swiping the screen left or right will switch to a different shooting mode.

• To access the camera's settings, press the Settings button.

2. Select ◯ Capture.

Configure recording mode

Facilitates the camera's ability to determine the optimal shooting mode or choose from a variety of options.

○ To change the shooting mode in the camera, merely swipe the screen left or right.

- Have fun: Use special Snapchat Lenses to change your look and your perspective on the world.

- If you're taking portraits, one tip is to change the background of your images.

- Allows the camera to choose the optimal settings for taking images.

- For videos, it lets the camera figure out what settings work best.

- Choose from several shooting modes that are easily accessible. To access the shooting modes tray at the bottom of your camera, press the plus sign.

- For the best results while shooting photos, use a manual exposure, white balance, ISO, and color tone adjustment.

- Macro: Get in close-up shots of objects by positioning yourself three to five centimeters away.

- For professional-quality videos, manually adjust the exposure value, white balance, color tone, and ISO sensitivity while recording.
- Take a number of still images and video clips from different perspectives in a single shot.
- Panoramic: Take images in either the vertical or horizontal plane to create a picture that runs horizontally.
- In low-light conditions, you can use this to take pictures without using the flash.
- Culinary: Snap photos that bring out the vibrant colors of the cuisine.
- For the best slow-motion experience, record videos at extremely high frame rates. After you've recorded a video, you can put it in slow motion and play back a specific segment.
- For slow-motion viewing, the slow motion feature records videos at extremely high frame rates.
- The Hyper lapse: Capture footage at multiple frame speeds to create time lapse movies. You can change the frame rate depending on the

scenario you're recording and how you're moving your smartphone.

AR Zone

Find all of the AR features in one convenient location.

○ Go to More in the Camera, and then tap AR Zone. The following functionalities are at your disposal:

- AR Emojis Studio: Create and personalize your very own My Emojis avatar with the help of the augmented reality tools.

- Make an avatar for yourself in My Emojis with the help of the AR Emojis Camera.

- The augmented reality emoji stickers: personalize your My Emojis avatar with these stickers.

- Using augmented reality doodles, you can easily add handwriting or line drawings to your environment, enhancing your movies. AR Doodle keeps an eye on your face and surrounding area to make sure they're moving with you.

- Deco Pic: Enhance live-streamed video or still images with the tap of a finger.

Record video

Use your device to record smooth, realistic videos.

1. Swiping left or right in Camera toggles the shooting mode to Video.

2. Press the ● Record button to begin filming.

- Press the Capture button to snap a photo while recording.

- Press ‖ Pause to temporarily halt recording.

  Press ● Resume to start recording again.

3. Once you've finished recording, touch Stop.

Camera settings

Make use of the icons located on the main camera screen and in the settings menu to adjust the camera's settings.

- o To access the following options in the Camera, tap Settings:

Smart functions

- Scenes optimizer: picture color settings are automatically adjusted to match the subject matter.

- Shot suggestions: Access on-screen guides to help you set up perfect shots.

- Automatically detect QR codes when using the camera for scanning.

Photo

- When you swipe the shutter to the farthest edge, you can choose to take burst images or create a GIF.

- To use the watermark, simply place it on the bottom left corner of your images.

- When you want to save space, one option is to save photos as very high efficiency pictures. It is possible that the format is incompatible with some sharing sites.

Selfie

- You can store selfies exactly as they appear in preview, without having to flip them.

Videos

- The High Efficiency Images: To save space, save photos as high efficiency images. It is possible that the format is incompatible with some sharing sites.

- Auto FPS: Video mode automatically optimizes frame rate, allowing you to record bright films even in low light.

- Video stabilization: To maintain focus stability even while the camera is moving, enable anti-shake.

Generally speaking

- Capture more detail in the light and dark areas of your photos with the help of automatic HDR.

- Grid lines: Display grid lines in the viewfinder to aid in picture or video composition.

- Location: Mark your photos and videos with a GPS location tag.

- Methods for shooting:

- You can use the volume buttons to regulate the system's volume, record videos, zoom in and out, and take pictures.

- Voice commands: Capture images while uttering important phrases.

- One such feature is the "Floating shutter key," which allows you to add a second shutter button and move it to any location on your screen.

- Show your hand: Extend your hand so that your palm is facing the camera. This will allow you to snap a photo quickly.

- Choose whether to launch Camera with the same photography options, angle, filters, and selfie as the last time by selecting the settings to remember.

- Storage location: Choose a place to keep your media files.

- To see the location of the storage, you'll need to insert the microSD card (not included).

- Shutter sound: Incorporate a musical tone into the photo-taking process.

- You can activate vibrations as a kind of feedback by touching the screen within the Camera app.

- If you want to add Snapchat filters and lenses to Fun mode, you can do that by activating this feature.

Other

- View Samsung's privacy information under the "Notice of Privacy" section.

- Permissions: Open the Camera app and access the necessary and optional permissions.

- Camera: View information about the app and software.

- Call Samsung's service line through Samsung's Member program to get in touch with us.

Gallery

You may see all of the pictures and videos stored on your device in the Gallery. Videos and photographs can be edited, viewed, and managed.

○ Select 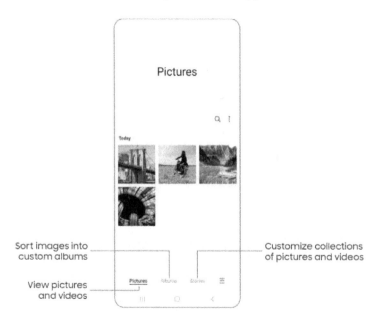 Gallery from the Applications menu.

Sort images into custom albums

View pictures and videos

Customize collections of pictures and videos

View pictures

The Gallery app allows you to view all of the pictures stored on your device.

1. Press on Pictures in the Gallery.

2. Press a picture to see it larger. To view further images or videos, simply swipe to the right or left.

- Pressing Bixby Vision will enable you to use it in this scenario.

- Click ♡ Add to the Favorites to make a photo a favorite.

- Select "More options" to gain access to the following features:

- See and change the photograph's information in the "Info" section.

- Remastering is the process of improving an image using built-in tools.

- You may add a portrait effect to your photos by adjusting the slider to either make the background less noticeable or more prominent.

- Pasting to the clipboard: cut the picture and paste it into another program.

- Make it your wallpaper: Choose a photo and make it your background.

- Transfer to Secure Folders: Transfer the images to the designated folders.

- Print: Copy an image to a connected printer.

Edit photos

Use Gallery's editing tools to elevate your images.

1. Select Pictures from the �֎ Gallery.

2. Simply touch an image to see it, and then press

    ✎ Edit to get the editing options listed below:

- Auto adjust: Use the auto adjust feature to improve the photo.

- ⛶ : Alter the overall look of your photo by using the "Transform" tool. This includes flipping, rotating, cropping, and more.

- ⬮: To apply color effects, use the filters.

- ☼ Tone: Adjust brightness, contrast, exposure, and more.

- ⋮ : You may see more editing possibilities here.

- You can get your original photo back by using the "Revert" button.

79

3. At the end, hit the Save button.

Play video

Play videos from your device's storage. You have the option to save videos to your favorites and examine their details.

1. Press on Pictures in the ✳ Gallery.

2. Just touch the video to watch it. To see more images or videos, swipe left or right.

- Select ♡ "Add to your Favorites" to save a video to a favorite list. After that, you can add that video to your Favorites in the Albums tab.

- Select "More options" to gain access to the following features:

- Details about the video can be seen and edited.

- Press the "Open on Video player" button to play the video in your default app.

- Make a movie the background of your lock screen by following these steps.

- Put this video into the designated folder for protected content.

3. To start playing the video, touch the Play video button.

Edit video

Use your device to edit videos that you have saved.

1. Select Pictures from the ✱ Gallery.

2. Click on a video to watch it.

3. To access the tools listed below, press ✎ Edit:

- 🔊: You may adjust the volume and even add music to your videos in the audio section.

- Press ▶ Play to see a preview of your finished videos.

- Trim the excess footage from your video.

- ⬜ Transform: Make global changes to the look of your films, such as flipping, cropping, rotating, and more.

- ◌ Filters: Enhance the videos with visual effects.

- Tones: Tone controls include exposure, brightness, contrast, and more.

- As for embellishments, you can use stickers, typography, or hand-drawn elements.

- View a wider range of editing possibilities.

- You can get your original video back by using the "Revert" button.

4. Select "Save" and then "Confirm" if asked.

Share videos and photos

Transfer media files between devices using the Gallery app.

1. Select Pictures from the ❄ Gallery.

2. Select the media files you want to share by tapping ⋮ More choices, then Edit.

3. To begin sharing, press Share, and then choose a network or app. Do as instructed.

Delete videos and photos

Get rid of all the photos and videos on your device.

1. Select ⋮ "More options" and then "Edit" under ❄ Gallery.

2. Click on images and videos to select them.

3. Select 🗑 Delete and then confirm when asked.

Group similar images together

In your Gallery, you can sort media files by how similar they are to one another.

1. Select "Group similar image" from the Gallery.

2. Revert to the default Gallery display by pressing the "Ungroup similar image" button.

Screenshot

To take a screenshot, just snap a picture of your screen. The Screenshots album will be automatically generated on the smartphone through the Gallery app.

- Side and volume down keys can be pressed and released on any screen.

Palm slide screenshot

Simply keep your hand in touch with the screen while swiping the edge of your hand from side to side to capture a screenshot.

1. To capture a palm swipe, go to the Settings menu, and then choose Advanced features. Then, tap on Motions & gestures. Finally, choose Palm swipe.

2. To activate this function, press ⬤.

Screenshot settings

You can change the settings for the screenshot.

- o Screenshots & screen recorder can be accessed in the ⬤ Advanced features section of the Settings menu.

- • After taking a screenshot, you can see more options in the display toolbar.

- • Screenshots immediately get erased after being shared through screenshot toolbars.

- • Avoid showing status bars and navigation on screenshots by hiding them.

- • Keep original screenshot: After making edits in the Gallery app, you can go back to the original screenshots.

- • Choose between PNG and JPG as the format for your screenshots.

- • Find the location where you want to save the screenshots.

Screen recorder

You may record your device's activity, jot down notes, and use the camera to capture a self-portrait overlay that you can then share with loved ones.

1. Select Screen Recorder from the Quick Settings menu.

2. Make your sound selection and then hit the "Start recording" button.

3. It starts recording after the three-second countdown. If you want to begin recording right away, you can use the Skip countdown button.

   - To start drawing on the screen, use the Draw button.

   - Tap on "Selfie videos" to include any footage captured by the front-facing camera.

4. To stop recording, use the Stop button. Your screen recordings will be immediately stored to the Screens album on Gallery.

Screen recorder settings

Manage the screen recorder's audio and quality settings.

- o To access the screen capture and recorder, go to the Settings menu, then tap on Advanced features.

- • The Sound: Use the screen recorder to choose which noises to capture.

- • Video resolution: Pick one. Increasing the resolution to achieve better quality will necessitate more space for storing.

- • To easily adjust the size of your video overlay, you can use the slider for selfies.

- • Display taps and touches: Enable this feature to customize the recording's screen taps and touches.

- • Save screen recording to: Decide where to save screen recordings.

Chapter Four
Applications

You can see all of the installed and preloaded apps in the Applications list. Both the Galaxy Store and Google Play allow users to easily download apps.

- To view the list of applications, just swipe up from the Home screen.

Disable or uninstall an application

Your device allows you to remove installed apps. It is only possible to disable certain preloaded apps that are accessible on your device by default. You can disable apps and hide them from the Applications list.

- Hold down an app in the Applications menu and then press Uninstall or Disable.

Search application

Use the Search function if you can't remember the name of an app or setting.

1. Input the word(s) in the search bar within the Apps. As you type, compatible apps and settings will appear as search results.

2. To access that app, touch any result.

Note: You may change your search preferences by going to ⋮ More options > Settings.

Sort applications

You have the option of using an alphabetical order or creating your own unique order for the shortcuts in the app.

- ○ To access the following sorting options in Applications, go to ⋮ More > Sort.

- • Personalization: Arrange applications by hand.

- • Application sorting by alphabetical order is one option.

Note: By selecting on ⋮ More options > then Clean up the pages, you may easily remove the empty icon gaps when programs are manually sorted (Custom order).

Create and use folders

You have the option to create folders in the Applications list to arrange app shortcuts.

1. To move an app shortcut from Applications to the top of another shortcut until it's

highlighted, hold down the shortcut and drag it.

2. The folder can be generated by releasing the application shortcut.

- Ensure that each folder is given a name.

- Palette: Change the color of the folder.

- ✛ : Put other apps on the folder by clicking the "Add applications" button. To select them, press the apps, and then hit the Done button.

3. To leave the folder, tap ‹ Back.

Copy folders to any home screen

To the Home screen, you can paste any folder.

○ To find a folder in the Apps, hold it down and then hit the ⊞ "Add to Home" button.

Delete any folder

Shortcuts to your apps will reappear in the Applications list after removing a folder.

1. Press and hold the folder in Applications to delete it.

2. Choose 🗑 Delete Folder and then "Confirm" when asked.

Game booster

Get top-notch gaming performance based on your usage. Turn on options that will improve your game experience and disable notifications.

o   To access the navigation bar while playing the game, slide up from the bottom of the screen. On the far left and right sides of the screen, you may see these options:

•   Touch protection: To prevent unintentional tapping, lock your screen. It's the one you're already using.

•   : With The Game Booster, you can customize your experience by enabling or disabling features like performance monitoring, screen captures, and screen touches.

Application settings

Oversee the uses of both installed and downloaded apps.

- o Select ⊞ Apps from the Settings menu. To make changes, tap the options:
- • Choose which apps to use for common tasks like sending messages, making calls, and accessing websites.
- • Samsung app settings: see all of your Samsung apps and adjust their settings to your liking.
- • Your apps: Select an app to see and change its usage and privacy settings information. Options could differ depending on the field.

Note: Use the "More options" menu item, then select "Reset application preferences," to erase all of your saved changes to an app's settings.

Calendar

The calendar app allows you to connect all of your internet accounts in one convenient location.

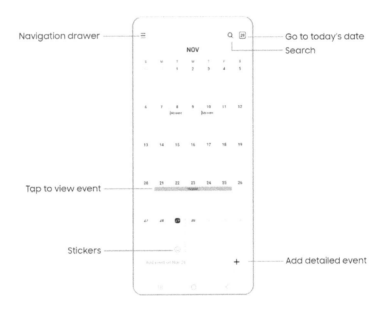

Add calendar

Your Calendar app allows you to add accounts.

1. Hit the ≡ Navigation drawer in 🗓 Calendar.

2. Go to Manage Calendars, then + Add Account and select the desired account type.

3. Following the on-screen instructions, enter your account details.

Note: Contacts, email, and other capabilities may be equally supported by accounts.

Calendar reminder style

You can customize the look of the alerts that come from your calendar app.

1. Press the ≡ Navigation drawer, then tap ⚙
    Calendar settings, and finally touch Alert style
    from within the 🔲 calendar application.

    You can access these choices below:

    *   Light: A notification and a short sound will be played.

    *   Medium: Hear a short sound and see the full-screen warnings.

    *   Alerts will be displayed in full screen and a ringtone will be heard until they are dismissed.

2. Here are some available sound selections based on the alert style selected above:

    *   Choose between a Medium or Light alarm type for the brief sound.

    *   Choose the Strong alerts style for the alerts sound in the Long menu.

Generate event

Put your Calendar to work for you by creating events.

1. To add the event, go to the Calendar and click on ⊕ Add comprehensive events.

2. Type in the details of your event and hit the "Save" button.

Delete event

The Calendar allows you to remove events.

1. You can edit an event by pressing it in the Calendar and then touching it again.

2. Select 🗑 Delete and then confirm when asked.

Chapter Five

Contact

Organize and store your contacts. Adding private accounts to the device allows you to sync with them. Calendars, emails, and other features can all be supported by accounts.

Create contact

1. To create a new contact, go to the  Contacts and tap ╬.

2. After you've entered your contact's information, hit the Save button.

Edit contact

Pressing a field while editing a contact allows you to delete or edit information and you may even add new fields to the contact's list of fields.

1. To access the contacts, choose one.

2. Choose Edit.

3. To edit, add, or remove data, simply touch any field.

4. Save the file.

Favorites

You may make all of your contacts easily available from any app by marking them as favorites. This will put them at the top of your contact lists.

1. Select a contact from the Contacts list.

2. Choose the "Favorites" button to save a contact.

• You can remove a contact from your Favorites by touching the Favorites button.

Share contacts

Various sharing platforms and ways make it easy to share contacts with others.

1. Select a contact from the Contacts list.

2. Click the ⌁ Share button.

3. Press on the Text or the vCard files (VCF).

4. Follow the on-screen instructions after selecting the sharing method.

Tip: You may easily exchange contact information with loved ones by tapping the ⋮ More menu, then QR code, while browsing any contact. As soon as you make a change to the available contact information, the QR code will reflect the change.

View contacts when sharing content

From within any program, you may send media files directly to contacts. When activated, the Share window will display your usual contacts.

o   To enable the option to display contacts when sharing material, go to Settings, tap on

Advanced features, and finally, tap ⬤ to activate.

Groups

Contacts can be organized using groups.

Create a group

Develop your own networks of personal contacts.

1. Select ☰ Show navigation menus > Groups from the ⬤ Contacts.

2. Then, fill out the group's details by pressing the Create group button and touching the fields:

*   Choose a name for your new group from the drop-down menu.

*   You can personalize the sounds that your group uses as its ringtone.

*   Select the contacts you wish to add to the new group, and then hit the "Done" button.

3. Save the file.

Delete or add group contact

You may edit the group by adding or removing contacts.

- o Click on ▬ Show navigation menus > Groups in the Contacts, and then select a group.

- • Press and hold the contact you want to remove before selecting 🗑 .

- • Click 🖊 Edit > Add the member, and then tap the contacts you wish to add. Select Done > Save when you're done.

Send message to group

The group's members might be contacted via text message.

1. Click on ▬ Show navigation menus > Groups in the 👤 Contacts, and then touch on a group.

2. To send a message, go to ⋮ More options > Send message.

Send email to group

It is possible to communicate with the group's members via email.

1. Select a group in Contacts by going to the menu and tapping on ▭ Show navigation menus > Groups.

2. Navigate to ⋮ More choices > Send email.

3. You can select many contacts at once by touching them, or you can select all at once by pressing the All checkbox in the top right of the screen, and then press Done.

    *   The display is limited to group members whose records contain email addresses.

4. Choose an email address and then follow the on screen instructions.

Delete group

A group you've created can be removed.

1. Press ▭ Show navigation menus > Groups from the 👤 Contacts screen, and then touch on a group.

2. Press the ⠿ "More options" button, and then proceed to delete the group.

- Select Delete just group to remove a specific group.

- You can eliminate a group and all of its contacts by selecting eliminate group and then dragging and dropping the members into the trash.

Merge contacts

Merge all of your contact information into one single record by linking entries into a single contact.

1. When you're in the ⬤ Contacts, go to the ☰ Show navigation menus > Manage contacts option.

2. Choose the "Merge contacts" option. We will group together all of the contacts whose names, email addresses, and phone numbers are identical.

3. Select the contacts by pressing on them, and then touch Merge.

Import contacts

A vCard file (VCF) is an option for importing contact information into the device.

1. Click on ☰ Show navigation menus > Manage contacts in the 👤 Contacts app.

2. Following the on-screen instructions, click the "Import contacts" button.

Export contacts

The vCard file (VCF) is an option for transferring contact information from the device.

1. Click on ☰ Show navigation menus > Manage contacts in the 👤 Contacts app.

2. Choose "Export contacts" and then follow the on-screen instructions.

Mobile contacts

Transferring contacts across devices and SIM cards is possible.

1. Click on ☰ Show navigation menus > Manage contacts in the 👤 Contacts app.

2. Click on Move contacts.

3. Press a location for From & To to transfer the contacts you've stored.

Sync contacts

Keep all of your contact information up-to-date across all of your accounts.

1. Select Manage contacts from the 👤 Contacts menu, and then choose ☰ Show navigation menus.

2. Find the Synchronize contacts button.

Delete contact

One or more contacts can be removed.

1. Press and hold the contacts to select them.

• Other contacts might also be selected for removal by touching them.

2. Select 🗑 Delete and then confirm when asked.

Emergency contact

Even when the device is locked, the emergency contacts can still be reached.

o Go to the Settings menu, and then choose 🔔
Safety & emergency. Then, choose Emergency contacts.

- Adding a member: Set up your phone's emergency contacts from the list of people you already have.

- Lock screen display: Put your emergency contacts front and center on your lock screen so you can quickly access them in an emergency.

Internet

Web browsing on your Samsung device has never been easier or faster than with Samsung's Internet. You can speed up your browsing, safeguard your privacy, and have a more secure online experience with these tools.

Browser tabs

You can open many websites at once by using tabs.

- From the ⬤ web, choose 1️⃣ Tabs > New Tab.

- Press 🔲 Tabs > ⊗ Close tab to close a specific tab.

Create bookmark

To quickly access the websites you like, you can bookmark them.

○ On the ◯ web, go to the page you want to save, and then click the ☆ "Add to bookmarks" button.

Open bookmark

Launch web pages quickly from the Bookmarks page.

1. Select ☆ Bookmarks from the ◯ Internet menu.

2. Find the bookmark and touch it.

Save page

When using the Samsung Internet app, you have multiple choices for saving a webpage.

○ Press ☰ "Tools" > "Add-page-to" from the ◯ Internet to see the following options:

- Bookmarks: Set up a list of websites to save for later.

- The Quick access: Get to the most often used or stored websites with ease.

- Make a shortcut to a website right from the Home screen.

- Stored pages: Make sure you can access webpage contents even when you're not connected to the internet by saving them to your device.

View history

To see a history of the websites you've visited:

o Go to the ⬤ Internet menu, select ☰ Tools, and finally, History.

Tip: To remove all traces of your web browsing, go to ⋮ More options > Clear history.

Share page

Websites can be shared with contacts.

○ Press ☰ Tools > tap Share from the ◐ Internet, and then follow the on-screen instructions.

Secret mode

If you visit a page in Secret mode, your browser and search history will not record it, and your device will not retain any traces of the page (such as cookies). The hue of the hidden tab is darker than that of the windows on the ordinary tab.

Even when you shut the hidden tabs, any files you downloaded will still be on your device.

1. Select ① Tabs > Enable Secret mode from the ◐ Internet.

2. To begin browsing in Secret mode, touch Start.

Secret mode settings

In order to access Secret mode, a password or biometric lock is required.

1. On the ◐ web, hit the ① tab key.

2. Select $\vdots$ "More options," then "Secret modes," to access the following options' settings:

- Use a password: Set one up to activate Secret mode and biometrics.

- Resetting Secret mode: Clear all data associated with Secret mode and return it to its default state.

Turn off secret mode

To go back to normal browsing, disable the Secret mode.

o   To disable the secret mode, go to the ⬭ Internet and press ① Tabs.

Internet settings

The Internet application's associated settings can be edited.

o   Once you're online, go to ☰ Tools > Settings.

Message

Use the Messages app to stay in touch with contacts easily by sending them photos, emojis, or a quick hello. The service providers differ in their options.

o Select "Compose new messages" from the  Messages menu.

Add an attachment ———   Record voice message

Message search

Using your search feature will help you find a message quickly.

1. Press   Search in   Messages.

2. To search, just type keywords into the search bar and press the Search key on your keyboard.

Delete conversation

Go ahead and delete the conversations to get rid of conversion histories.

1. You can delete messages from the Messages app by going to More > Delete.

2. Select each conversation you wish to remove by touching on it.

3. When asked, press "Delete all," and then confirm.

Emergency messaging

Your emergency contacts can receive messages that include audio and pictures.

1. Press your button five times to activate the following features: Go to Settings, and then choose Safety & emergency, and finally, Emergency SOS.

- Choose the amount of seconds to wait before activating emergency actions using the countdown.

- Select contact numbers to use in the event of an emergency.

- Enable location sharing with emergency contacts: Turn this feature on to let them know where you are.

Note: An alternate method of activating the emergency SOS is to press the side and volume down buttons simultaneously, followed by the emergency call button.

Message settings

Modify the preferences for text messages and multimedia.

- o Press ⋮ More options > Settings from the 💬 Messages.

Emergency alerts

These alert you to impending dangers and other events. Emergency alerts can be received at no cost.

Choose Wireless-Emergency-Alerts from the

Safety & emergency menu in Settings to personalize
your alert notifications.

Note: The Notifications tab is also where you can

access the emergency alerts. Press Notifications in
Settings, then tap Advanced Settings, and finally
choose Wireless-Emergency-Alerts.

My File

Get to and organize all of the media files (movies, photos, music, and sound clips) stored on your device. Accessing and managing files saved to cloud accounts is just as easy.

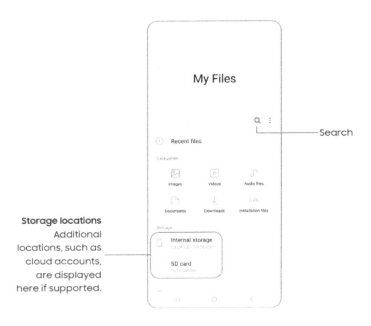

Storage locations
Additional locations, such as cloud accounts, are displayed here if supported.

Search

File groups

Here is a hierarchy of the file types saved on your device:

- Files accessed recently: View the files that were accessed recently.

- If a file has been viewed recently, this option will be displayed.

- Files can be viewed in different categories based on their type.

- The Storage: Access the files saved on your device's cloud storage and, if you have one, its optional SD card.

- The specifics of your cloud account might change depending on the apps you use.

- In the trash, you can choose to restore accidentally deleted files or delete them permanently.

- Looking at storage: Find out what's taking up room on the storage.

My File settings

This is a great tool for personalizing file management settings and more. Each service provider has their own set of options.

- To access the settings for these options, go to My Files, and then click More options.

- Accounts in the cloud: Access and manage cloud services.

- You can personalize the process of deleting, viewing, and accessing files in the mobile data management section.

- While analyzing storage, choose the file size to flag before continuing.

- Privacy: Controlling who can access My-Files.

Telephone

Using an app on a smartphone is useful for much more than just making calls. Take a look at the more advanced calling features.

Phone call

From various places on your smartphone, including the Home screen, Contacts, and the Recents tab, you can make and receive calls using the app.

Make a call

From the Home screen of your smartphone, you can make and answer calls.

- o Select 📞 Call from the 📞 Phone menu after entering a number using your keypad.
- • If your keypad isn't visible, touch it.

Make a call using Recent Calls

The call log keeps track of all incoming, outgoing, and missed calls.

1. To view a list of recent calls, go to 📞 Phone and hit Recents.

2. To make a call, touch the contact and then hit 📞.

Using your Contacts to make calls

Right from the Contacts app, you can dial a number to reach your contact.

- o To dial a contact's number, just drag your finger from the left side of their contact to the right in Contacts.

118

Answer a call

The phone rings and the caller's name or number shows on the screen whenever a call comes in. When a call comes in while you're using an app, a pop-up window will appear.

  o If you want to answer a call that comes in, you can do it by dragging the 📞 Answer button to the right side of the screen.

Note: In order to answer an incoming call, simply press the 📞 Answer button on the pop-up screen.

Reject a call

It is possible to reject any incoming call at any time. As you continue to use that app, the pop-up window for the incoming call will appear.

  o To reject the call and send it to voicemail, slide the 📞 Decline button to the left on the incoming call screen.

Note: Use the 📞 Decline button on the incoming call pop-up screen to put the call into voicemail and reject it.

Reject call and leave a message

Responding to incoming calls using text message is an option.

- o Choose a message and slide the Send message up button on the screen that appears when a call comes in.

Tip: Select a message and hit Send on the pop-up screen that appears when you receive an incoming call.

End call

- o Select ⏺ "End call" when you are prepared to terminate the call.

Actions during a telephone conversation

It was possible to multitask while on the phone, change the call's volume, and switch between speaker and headphone.

- o To adjust the level of sound, press and hold the volume buttons.

Switch to speaker or headphones

Use the built-in speaker or a Bluetooth headset (not provided) to listen to incoming calls.

o To hear a caller through the speaker, touch the

 ◁)) Speaker icon. To hear a caller through a

 Bluetooth headset, touch the ✳ Bluetooth

 icon.

Multitasking

Your active calls are seen in the status bar when you close the call screen to utilize another app.

To return to the call screen, do the following:

o Touch the call; slide the status bar downward to see the notification window.

If you're trying to end a call while multitasking, you can accomplish it like this:

o Pull down the status bar to see the notification pane; from there, tap ⌒ End call.

Call background

When you make or receive a phone call, you can choose to display a video or photo.

o Choose ⋮ "More options" from the 🅒 Phone's menu, then "Settings." Provides context for the following choices:

- Layout: decide how to show the caller's information if they have a profile picture.

- Background: Pick a picture to show off while you're on the phone.

Incoming call pop-up settings

It is possible for calls to appear as pop-ups when other apps are being used.

o Press More choices > touch Settings > then in the 🅒 Phone. Use the call screen while interacting with apps. You can access the following options:

- Opens the phone app in full screen mode, where incoming calls are displayed.

- Miniature window: A window will appear in the top right corner of your screen to display any incoming calls.

- Mini pop-ups: Show incoming calls in a more compact format.

- If you'd like to retain incoming calls in your pop-up window even after you've answered them, you can enable this feature.

Manage calls

Your phone conversations are being logged on the call log. Call records, voicemail, and speed dials are all at your fingertips.

Call log

Your call log keeps track of all the calls you've made, received, or missed.

- Press Recents on the 🄲 Phone. A record of all your recent phone conversations is shown. The name of the caller is displayed when they are in your Contacts list.

Save contacts from recent calls

Use the information from a recent call to add or modify contacts.

1. Find Recents in your 🄲 Phone's menu.
2. Select the call whose details you wish to add to your contacts by pressing the corresponding button.
3. Touch You can either add new contacts or edit the ones you already have.

Delete call record

To remove items from the call log:

1. Choose Recents from the Phone's menu.

2. Click and hold the call you want to delete from your call history.

3. Hit delete.

Block a number

When a caller is added to your Block lists, any future calls from that number will be directed to voicemail and you will not get any messages from them.

1. Reach out and touch Recents on your Phone.

2. The second step is to add a caller to your block list by touching on them and then pressing Details.

3. Hit Block or More > then tap Block contact and confirm if asked.

Note: In the Settings menu, you'll also find the option to edit your Block lists. Press the More options button on the Phone, then touch Settings. From there, choose Block numbers.

Speed Dial

A contact's default number can be quickly dialed using the Speed dial shortcut.

1. Keypad > More options > Speed dial number is the first option while using the Phone. You can see the reserved speed dial numbers on the screen of your speed dial number.

2. Feel free to touch the number that has not yet been assigned.

•   Instead of pressing the next number in the sequence, press ▼ Menu to select a different Speed-dial number.

•   The first one is just for voicemail.

3. The third step is to assign a contact to a number by entering the number or by tapping the Add from the Contacts button.

•   In the "Speed dial numbers" box, you can see the selected contact.

125

Make a call using speed dial

You can use the speed dial to make a call.

o While on the phone, keep your finger on the speed dial button.

• To input a Speed-dial number that is at least one digit long, press and hold the last digit while entering the first digit.

Delete speed dial number

Any assigned speed dial number can be removed.

1. Go to the ⚫ Phone menu, and then select ⋮ More options. Then, choose Speed-dial numbers.

2. To remove a contact from the speed dial, just press the ▬ Delete button next to their name.

Emergency calls

In your area, dialing the emergency cell phone number will get you through regardless of your cell phone's service state. Your phone can only be used for emergency calls when it is deactivated.

1. Press the call button after entering the emergency cell phone number (9-1-1 in North America).

2. Finish the call. You can use most of the in-call functions while on this type of call.

Note: Even if your phone is locked, anyone can dial the emergency number, so your phone can still be used to call for help in an emergency. If the caller were to access the locked screen directly, they would only be able to use the emergency calling features. The remainder of the mobile device is safeguarded.

Phone settings

You can use them to change preferences for your phone app.

o   Click on "More options" and then "Settings" on the Phone.

Optional calling services

Future phone calls may be possible depending on your cellphone operator and plan.

Call multiple participants

While one call is in progress, make more calls. Each service provider has their own set of possibilities.

1. To make a second call, go to your active call and tap ┼ on Add phone call.

2. Dial a fresh number and press 📞 Call. When a caller answers, you can switch between them by pressing the ⬚ "Switch" or "On-hold" button.

- To listen to both callers simultaneously (multi-conferencing), press the ⤻ Merge button.

Video call

For video conferencing:

o Once you've entered a number, press the 🄲 Phone button and then choose 🎥 Meet or ○ / 🎥 Video calls.

Note: This video calling feature is not compatible with all devices. In other words, the receiver can choose to treat this video call like any other call, or they can ignore it entirely.

Video call effect

In some of the apps, you may change the background color or even blur it while a video call is in progress.

1. Select Video call's effects from the
   Advanced features section of the Settings menu.

2. Activate this function with a touch.

3. Pick an accessible choice:

- You have the option to have the virtual background turned into a solid color automatically depending on your surroundings.

- Choose an image from your photo library to use as the backdrop for your video conversations.

Wireless calling

Carry on a phone conversation while linked to a Wi-Fi network.

1. Press More choices on the Phone. Then, touch Settings. Finally, choose Wi-Fi calling.

2. Turn this function by tapping .

3. Follow the on-screen instructions to set up and setup your Wi-Fi calling.

Real Time Text (RTT)

With Real-Time Text (RTT), you and another person can input and receive text messages in real-time while on the phone.

When making a call to someone whose smartphone is RTT-compatible or has a teletypewriter (TTL) device connected, you can use RTT. When an RTT phone call comes in, you'll see the RTT icon.

1. Press More options > Settings on the Phone.

2. To access the following options, press Real-time-text:

- For your RTT call key, you can adjust the visibility settings.

- Concealed throughout the calls: During calls only, display the RTT call key.

- Keep it visible: Show the RTT call key on your keypad and when you're on the phone.

• If you're using external TTY keyboards, you should conceal your RTT keyboard at all times.

• TTY modes: Set the target TTY modes for the currently active keyboards.

Samsung Health

Utilize Samsung's Health to organize and track several elements of daily living that impact well-being, including as food, exercise, and sleep.

Note: The data collected from the device, Samsung Health, or any related apps should not be used for medical diagnosis, treatment, prevention, or mitigation purposes.

The information and data provided by this device and its software could be impacted by factors such as the surrounding environment, specific actions taken while wearing or using the device, device settings, user configuration or data provided by the user, and various interactions with the end user.

Before beginning a workout

You should always consult your doctor before starting an exercise program, even though Samsung's Health app is a great ally on the journey. Although little exercise, such as brisk walking, is perfectly safe for some people, doctors advise against starting any kind of fitness program without first discussing it with your doctor, especially if you suffer from any of the following conditions:

- Diseases of the heart, lungs, liver, kidneys, diabetes, and arthritis are all on the list.

If you have any symptoms that could indicate a serious illness, such as those related to the heart, lungs, or other major organs, such as: see your doctor before beginning an exercise program.

Consult your physician or other qualified medical professional before beginning any new workout program. Before starting any new workout program, you should consult your doctor, especially if you are pregnant, have any preexisting conditions, or are unsure of your current health state.

Samsung Notes

You may use Samsung Notes to make audio recordings, add music, text, and photographs with captions. Using social networking services, sharing your notes is a breeze.

Make use of these to compose a message that incorporates audio recordings, visuals with captions, and text. Sharing the notes with a social media platform is a breeze.

Create a note

Include media such as pictures, text, audio, and more.

1. Hit the ⓔ Add button in 🔲 Samsung Notes.

2. Make use of the text tools at your disposal to craft your content.

Voice recording

Make meeting or lecture-ready annotated voice recordings. Remember to take notes as you record audios. The playback is timed so that you can jump to the relevant text.

1. Press the ⓔ Add button in 🔲 Samsung Notes.

2. Next, choose Voice recording from the 📎 Insert menu.

3. When you're recording audio, make use of the text options to add content.

Edit notes

Edit the notes you've already written.

1. To access a note in 🔲 Samsung Notes, simply touch on it.

2. To make changes, touch ⬚ Edit.

3. When you're ready, hit ⟨ the button to go back.

Note option

The notes can be sorted, edited, or managed in any way you like.

The following options can be accessed via the ⬚ Samsung Notes:

○ ⬚ : Open a PDF file in Samsung Notes and then import it.

• ⬚ Find the keyword using the search.

• ⬚ Additional options:

- In the "Edit" menu, you can select notes to delete, distribute, save as a file, relocate, or unlock.

- Change the view to List, Grid, or Simple lists.

- Keep the notes you've marked as favorites near the top of your main page by pinning them.

Notes menu

Sorting notes by category is all that's required.

○ Press the ☰ "Show navigation menus" button in the ⬛ Samsung Notes app to get the following options:

* ⚙ Preferences for Samsung Notes: Find the preferences for your Samsung Notes app.

* Each and every note: View every note.

* Shared notebook: Access shared notebooks with contacts through Samsung's account.

* Trash: Recover notes that have been erased up to 15 days ago.

* Get a bird's-eye view of your notes by folder.

* Organize and manage your folders: create, remove, and rename them.

Chapter Six
Access Settings

There are multiple ways to access your device's settings.

- To access the settings, just slide down from the home screen and hit ⚙ .

- Choose ⊙ Settings from the Applications menu.

Search settings

You can use the search function when you don't know the exact location of a setting.

1. Press 🔍 Search in Settings and enter keywords.

2. Press the enter key to navigate to that specific option.

Connections

You have the ability to control the connections between your device and other networks and other devices.

Wi-Fi

Without utilizing mobile data, you can still browse the Internet by connecting your device to a Wi-Fi network.

1. Press ⬤▭ to activate Wi-Fi and search for accessible networks in Settings; then, go to 📶Connections and tap Wi-Fi.

2. Enter a password when prompted after touching a network.

3. Click the Connect button.

Connect to a hidden Wi-Fi network

You can still connect to the required Wi-Fi network by manually entering its details, even if it isn't listed after the scan. Preparation is key, so get the name and password from the Wi-Fi network administrator.

1. Press ⬤ to enable Wi-Fi after going to Settings > 🛜 Connections > Wi-Fi.

2. Press ➕ the "Add network" button at the very bottom of the list.

3. Punch in details regarding wireless networks:

- Enter the exact name of the network.

- Security: Select the appropriate security settings from the drop-down menus and enter the password when prompted.

- The password for the network must be entered.

- Concealed networks: Include a hidden network.

- More viewing options: specify sophisticated settings like IP and proxy.

4. Save the file.

Tip: In order to connect to a Wi-Fi network, all you have to do is use your device's camera to scan the QR codes. Just press the ⌗ "Scan QR codes" button.

Intelligent Wi-Fi settings

You can manage stored networks, find your device's network address, and connect to various types of Wi-Fi networks and hotspots. Each service provider has their own set of possibilities.

1. You may activate Wi-Fi by going to the Settings menu, selecting ⛅ Connections, tapping Wi-Fi, and finally pressing ⬭.

2. Simply touch Intelligent Wi-Fi under ⋮ "More options" to access the following:

- When your Wi-Fi signal drops, your device will automatically switch to mobile data if this feature is turned on. It returns to the Wi-Fi when the signal strength is high.

- Automatically moving to better Wi-Fi networks: Move to Wi-Fi networks that are more stable or much quicker.

- Have Wi-Fi turned on or off automatically: Turn on Wi-Fi in the places you use it most.

- Show network quality data: Include network data (such as stability and speed) in the available Wi-Fi network lists.

- Get alerts if the current Wi-Fi network exhibits questionable behavior by using the feature that identifies potentially malicious networks.

- Connect to Wi-Fi hotspots immediately when they are discovered.

- Access versions of Intelligent Wi-Fi through the Intelligent Wi-Fi.

Advanced Wi-Fi settings

Access a variety of Wi-Fi networks and hotspots, manage stored networks, and find your device's network addresses are all within your reach. Each service provider has their own set of possibilities.

1. Press to enable Wi-Fi after going to Settings > Connections > Wi-Fi.

2. For the following choices, tap "More options" and then "Advanced."

- If you have an account with Samsung, you can sync your Wi-Fi profiles with their cloud service.

- Notify me that the Wi-Fi is available when I run programs by showing the Wi-Fi pop-up.

- Wi-Fi or network notifications: Receive alerts anytime nearby open networks are detected.

- Network management: View saved Wi-Fi networks and chooses to automatically rejoin to or forget each one.

- The apps that have turned your Wi-Fi on or off recently: See which apps have done this.

- Connect mechanically to Wi-Fi networks that are compatible with Hotspot 2.0.

- Authentication certificate installation: install your authentication certificates on the network.

Direct Wi-Fi

All it does is use Wi-Fi to transfer files across different devices.

1. To enable Wi-Fi, go to the Settings menu, select 🛜 Connections, touch Wi-Fi, and finally push ⬭.

2. Next, choose Wi-Fi Direct from the list of possibilities.

3. Simply touch a device and follow the on-screen instructions to establish a connection.

Disconnect Wi-Fi Direct

Remove your device from the Wi-Fi Direct device.

○ To access Wi-Fi Direct, go to Settings, then tap 🛜 Connections, then Wi-Fi. Press More choices, and finally, Wi-Fi Direct. Simply touching an item will turn it off.

Bluetooth

Connecting your device to other Bluetooth-enabled devices is as easy as pairing your headphones with your car's infotainment system. When devices are paired, they remember each other and can share data without having to enter the passkey again.

1. To activate Bluetooth, go to Settings, press 📶 Connections, touch Bluetooth, and finally touch ⬭.

2. Reach out and connect at the touch of a button.

- Press Disconnect to end the pairing with the linked device. Tap on Connect to establish a connection.

Note: You can use this feature by tapping the Bluetooth icon while sharing any file.

Rename paired device

To facilitate identification, you can rename the paired device.

1. To activate Bluetooth, go to Settings > 📶 Connections > Bluetooth, and finally, press ⬭.

2. Select Rename from the ⚙ Settings menu that appears next to the device name.

3. Touch the Rename button after entering the new name.

Unpairing a Bluetooth device

When you unpair from a Bluetooth device, the two devices stop recognizing each other and you have to pair them again before you can connect to them.

1. To activate Bluetooth, go to the Settings menu, select Connections, touch Bluetooth, and finally press .

2. Hit the Settings button next to your gadget, and then hit the Unpair button.

3. To confirm, just touch Unpair.

Advanced Bluetooth settings

In the Advanced menu, you'll find more Bluetooth options.

1. Select Bluetooth after tapping Connections from Settings.

2. To access the following options, go to the Advanced settings menu, select More choices, and finally, the Advanced setting:

- Link up with Samsung's cloud service or account: Link up files shared by Bluetooth with Samsung's cloud service or account.

- The name of the device used for Bluetooth connections can be changed.

- Files Received: View collections of files received using Bluetooth.

- If you have a Bluetooth speaker or headphones, you can share music with your buddies.

- Harmonization of ringtones: When you get calls on the connected Bluetooth device, play the ringtones you've previously set.

- You can see which apps have lately utilized Bluetooth in the Bluetooth control history.

- Adding devices that prevent pairing requests is an option.

- You can modify the Bluetooth settings for apps and see which ones have recently searched for nearby Bluetooth devices in the Bluetooth scan histories.

Dual audio

Two Bluetooth audio devices can be connected to your device so you can play music wirelessly.

1. Connect audio devices to the device over Bluetooth.

2. Select Media output from the Notifications panel.

3. Press the button next to each audio device (about two) in the Audio output to play music to them.

Near Field Communication (NFC) and Payments

You can interact with other devices even when you're not connected to the internet thanks to Near Field Communication (NFC). Some payment apps and the Android Beam both use this same technique. You can't send anything until the receiving device has NFC capability and is within 4 cm of it.

o   To enable this option, go to Settings, press Connections, touch NFC and contactless payments, and finally push   .

Click and pay

You can pay with just a touch of your phone to a credit card reader that supports near field communication (NFC) apps.

Tap your device to a compatible credit card reader to complete a purchase using an NFC payment app.

1. To activate NFC, go to Settings > Connections > NFC and contactless payments, and finally hit ⬭.

2. View your default payment app with a touch of the Contactless payment button.

- Select another payment app by tapping on one that is already available.

- A payment app can be used by touching the Pay button while the app is open.

- To change the default payment service, go to Others and then tap on the provider you like.

Airplane

By doing so, you cut off all access to the internet and any wireless or mobile data networks, including Bluetooth, Wi-Fi, and messaging. After you've toggled

Airplane mode on, you can turn on Wi-Fi and Bluetooth in the Settings or by going to the Quick Settings window.

o To activate this option, go to Settings, and then tap on Connections. Then, touch on Airplane mode. Finally, push .

Note: There may be regulations and restrictions imposed by municipal and federal authorities regarding the use of portable electronic devices on board ships and airplanes. By switching to airplane mode, all network connectivity would be disabled. You can disable ultra-wideband by switching to aircraft mode, which is required for ships and airplanes. Before using your device, make sure you've consulted the appropriate authorities and that you're following the crew's directions.

Mobile network

To enable your device to connect to mobile networks and make use of mobile data, you should use mobile networks. Each service provider has their own set of possibilities.

- To access mobile networks, go to Settings and select 📶 Connections.
- Turn on mobile data usage the mobile data.
- Adjust the settings for international data roaming, which includes voice, messages, and data.
- Data roaming: Set your device's settings to allow or disallow access to mobile data while you're outside your service provider's network area.
- Access to mobile networks while roaming can be configured in the data's roaming settings.
- Network modes: Your mobile device gives you the option to select which network mode it can use.
- Access Point Names (APNs): Choose or create the APNs that include the provider-specific network configurations that your device needs to connect.
- Network operators: choose preferred and available networks.

- Mobile network diagnostics: gather diagnostic and usage data for troubleshooting purposes.

- Scan for cells that can extend the network connection; they are networks extenders.

- Managing the connection settings that could affect your monthly costs is made easier with the help of these capabilities.

Mobile hotspot

This creates a Wi-Fi network that many devices can connect to by utilizing the data plans.

1. Select Mobile hotspot & tethering from the Connections menu in Settings, and then tap Mobile hotspot.

2. To enable the mobile hotspot, press the button.

3. Turn on Wi-Fi and select your mobile hotspot on the devices you want to link. Next, connect to the mobile hotspot by entering its password.

- Under the heading "Connected devices," you'll see a list of all the connected devices.

Tip: An alternative to entering a password is to press and hold a QR code; this will allow you to connect another device to the mobile hotspot.

Set mobile hotspot settings

The mobile hotspot's security and connection settings are up for grabs.

1. Select Mobile hotspot & tethering from the 📶Connections menu in Settings, and then tap Mobile hotspot.

2. To change the following settings, press Configure:

- Name of the network: You may see and alter the name of your mobile hotspot.

- Password: You can access or modify the password for any security level that uses it.

- Band: Choose one of the available bandwidth options.

- Safety: Set the mobile hotspots' security level.

- Advanced: Customize additional options for the mobile hotspot.

Auto hotspot

Allow additional devices linked to your Samsung account to automatically share your hotspot's connection.

1. To access mobile hotspot and tethering, go to Settings > Connections > Mobile hotspot & tethering.

2. To enable this feature, press and hold the "Auto hotspot" button.

Tethering

Using tethering, you can connect many devices to your device's Internet connection. Each service provider has their own set of possibilities.

1. Access mobile hotspot and tethering by going to Settings > Connections.

2. Select an option:

- To connect another device to your Internet network using Bluetooth, just touch the "Bluetooth tethering" button.

- Use a USB cable to link your computer to your device, and then enable USB tethering.

- Press the Ethernet tethering button after you've connected your computer to your device through the Ethernet adapter.

Ethernet

You can connect your device to any local network using the Ethernet connector in case your wireless network connection isn't working.

1. Attach an Ethernet cable to your device.

2. Follow the on-screen instructions after selecting Connections from the Settings menu. Then, go to More connection settings and select Ethernet.

Note: To connect Ethernet wires to your device, you will need an adapter, which is not provided.

Unblock the network

Check the device's network lock status and see if it's eligible to be unlocked so you can use it on other mobile networks. Each service provider has their own set of possibilities.

o Select Networks unlock for the following options from the ⬤ Connections menu in Settings:

- Get the current status of your device's network lock with the help of the Networks lock status.

- Get your device unlocked permanently so you can use it with the other network provider.

- One option is to temporarily unlock your networks so you can continue using your device with your other service provider.

Connect devices

Get mobile connectivity on all of your devices and any others you have linked. Each service provider has their own set of possibilities.

o Press ⬤ Connected Gadgets in the Settings menu to get the following features:

- Quick exchange: Anyone with a Samsung account can easily exchange documents and files with your device.

- Auto-switching Buds: Whenever you answer the phone, make a call, or play music, this device will immediately swap out your other Galaxy Buds for these.

- Using the Galaxy devices you have connected to your Samsung account, you can make and receive calls as well as send and receive text messages on other devices.

- Pick up where you left off on other devices by logging in with your Samsung account on Galaxy devices.

- Connecting to Windows: Connect your device to your Windows PC so you can access all of your photos, messages, and more right away.

- Multi control: Use the Galaxy Book's keyboard and cursor to navigate this gadget and move stuff around.

- Smart Views: Display the device's screen or play a video on a nearby TV.

- Galaxy Wearable: Pair your device with your Samsung watch or earphones.

157

- SmartThings: Connect your device to a network of advanced home automation systems.

- To keep your hands free for the road, use Android Auto to sync your phone with compatible vehicle screens.

Sound and vibration

Notifications, screen touches, and other interactions may be specified through vibrations and sounds that you could control.

Sound mode

You don't need to use the volume keys to switch between different sound modes on your smartphone.

- To change the mode, go to the Settings menu, and then tap on 🔊 Sounds & vibration.

- Sound: For alerts and notifications, utilize the vibrations, noises, and volume levels you've chosen in the Sounds settings.

- Make the device vibrate in addition to ringing when you receive a call.

- To get alerts and notifications, just use the vibration feature.

- Mute: Turn device off so it doesn't make a sound.

- You can temporarily silence your device by setting a time limit.

Note: If you want to change the sound mode without adjusting the volume, here's a hint: use the mode slider instead.

Mute with gesture

Quickly silence your device by covering the screen or turning it upside down.

○ To enable the ability to mute using gestures, go to the Settings menu, select Advanced features, touch Motions & gestures, and finally, touch .

Vibration

When and how your device vibrates are under your control.

1. Select Sounds & vibration from the Settings menu.

2. Access personalization options with a touch:

- For incoming calls, you can choose from a variety of vibrating patterns that have been pre-set.

- Vibration for notifications: Choose a pattern from the ones already set.

- Vibration in the system: Set the feedback and vibration intensity for the following options:

  - You can adjust the system's vibration strength by dragging the slider.

  - Touch interactions: vibrates in response to screen touches (such as navigation keys or items held down).

  - If your phone has a dial pad, it will vibrate anytime you press a number.

  - When you type on a Samsung keyboard, it makes a vibrating sound.

  - When the charger is attached, it will vibrate to indicate charging.

  - When you use the navigation gestures, it vibrates.

- Camera's feedback: Snaps, zooms, and changes photography modes, among other things.

• The Vibration intensity: With the use of sliders, you may adjust the level of vibration for calls, notifications, and touch interactions.

Volume

Ringtones, media, notifications, and system noises can all have their volume levels adjusted.

o You can adjust the volume of each sound by dragging the corresponding sliders in the Sounds & vibration section of the Settings menu.

Tip: The Volume buttons work just as well for this purpose. When you press it, a menu will appear that shows you the current sound kind and volume level. You can touch the menus to expand them, and you can drag the sliders to alter the loudness of different types of sounds.

Using the media volume buttons

Instead of controlling the volume of the currently playing sound, you can set the volume buttons to control the volume of your media.

1. Select Volume from the 🔊 Sounds & vibration menu in Settings.

2. To activate the feature, press the Use Volume buttons for media.

Media volume limit

Limit the highest volume your device may go while using the headphones or Bluetooth speakers (not included).

1. Navigate to 🔊 Sounds & vibration > Volume in the Settings menu.

2. Select Media Volume Limit from the ⋮ More options menu.

3. To activate this function, press 　.

• Drag the Custom volumes limit slider to set the maximum output volumes.

- To enter a PIN in order to modify the volume, press the Set volumes limit PIN button.

Ringtone

Simply choose from the preset sounds or add your own to personalize the call's ringtone. Each service provider has their own set of possibilities.

1. Select Ringtone from the 🔊 Sounds & vibration menu in Settings.

2. The volume of your ringtone can be adjusted by dragging the slider.

3. To preview and select a ringtone, touch on it.

   Alternatively, you can tap ➕ Add to use audio files as ringtones.

Notification sound

With the notification alerts, you can choose from a variety of pre-set sounds.

1. To adjust the sound for notifications, go to the Settings menu, and then choose 🔊 Sounds & vibration.

2. The loudness of the notice can be adjusted by using the slider.

3. You can listen to a preview and choose it by touching the sound.

Note: You may also change the tone of the notifications so they are unique for each app under the settings menu of the application.

Notification

By changing the apps that deliver notifications and the way they inform you, you may simplify and organize your application alerts.

App notification

Select which application can send you notifications.

○ To enable notifications for individual apps, go to Settings, then tap Notifications > Application notifications and tap .

Lock screen notification

Make a selection on the Lock screen on which alerts are acceptable.

o To activate the feature, go to Settings, press

   ⬛Notifications, touch Lock screen's

   notifications, and finally, push ⬤ .

   Customize with the touch of a button:

- Keep items hidden: Your Notification pane will
  not show any notifications.

- Reveal content: The Notification pane will
  show any notifications.

- Show contents when unlocked: When the
  screen is not locked, display the contents of
  any notifications.

- Choose which notifications to show on the
  lock screen under the "Notifications to display"
  option.

- The ability to show notifications on the
  Always-On-Display screen is available as an
  option.

Notification popup style

You have more control over the notifications and can
modify their style.

○ To access the notification pop-up styles, go to the Settings menu, press Notifications, tap Notifications pop-up style, and finally, choose one:

- Quick: Turn on the ability to personalize the alerts.
- Apps to show as short notifications: Choose which apps will show as short notifications.
- You may customize the edge's lighting to show notifications in a variety of styles.
- If you have a lot of important keywords in your notifications, you can color them according to your preferences.
- Show notifications even when screen is off: You can decide whether to show notifications even when screen is off.
- Detailed: Turn on the Samsung Notifications settings that come standard.

Do not disturb

When this mode is turned on, you can easily disable notifications and audio. Apps, persons, and alarms could all be marked as exceptions. Regular occurrences, like meetings or sleep cycles, might also have their own schedules.

o Press Notifications > Do-not-disturb in Settings, and then configure the following:

- To silence incoming calls and other notifications, just toggle the "Do-not-disturb" switch to the "on" position.

- What is the length of time? Whenever you manually activate Do-not-disturb mode, choose the default timeframe.

Schedules

- While you sleep, you can set your device to automatically go into Do-not-disturb mode.

- Schedule addition: Create new schedules to establish regular times and days to place your device into Do-not-disturb mode.

Enabled when in the "Do-not-disturb" mode

- For calls and messages, touch to enable the Do-not-disturb feature.

- You can customize the Do-not-disturb mode by adding programs that you would like to get notifications from. Even if you disable the apps that are associated with a message, call, or discussion, you will still receive notifications about them.

- Sounds and alarms: When Do-not-disturb mode is still active, you can activate the sounds and vibrations for events, alarms, and reminders.

- Hiding notifications: Go to the settings menu and find the option to hide notifications.

Advanced notification settings

The alerts that services and applications send you could be set up.

o Select Notifications from the Settings menu, and then go to Advanced settings.

- Change the amount of notifications shown on the status bar by displaying the icons for each.

- Show the current percentage of battery life on your device's status bars.

- Notification histories: Show both recently received and snoozed alerts.

- Conversations: Get notifications for conversations. To make a chat mute, alert, or prioritize it, hold down its notification.

- You can enable floating notifications on the Smart pop-up view or the Bubbles view.

- Suggest responses and activities for notifications: Get relevant options for your notification and message replies and actions.

- To quickly snooze notifications, activate the feature that shows the snooze button.

- You can enable and personalize the periodic reminders on alerts from selected services and apps in the "Notifications" section. Stop receiving reminders by clearing the notifications.

- Badges on app icons: Show which apps have a lot of activity by adding badges to their icons. Find out how many unread alerts you have by touching the badges.

- You may personalize your emergency alert notifications with the wireless feature.

Notifications when picking up the smartphone

When you pick up the phone, your device can vibrate to let you know that you have incoming calls or texts.

- o If you want to activate the feature that notifies you when your smartphone is picked up, go to the Settings menu, press on Advanced features, then touch Motions & gestures.

Display

In addition to adjusting the timeout delay, text size, and brightness of your screen, you have access to a plethora of other display settings.

Dark mode

By dimming the white or bright panels and notifications, you can switch to a darker theme that will be much easier on the eyes at night.

- o To access the following options, go to Settings and then press Display:

- Light: Set the device to its default light color theme.

- Dark: Just give the device a black theme.

- Dark Mode Settings: Control the application of Dark mode and when it activates.

- Turn on at the appointed time: You can configure the Sunset-to-sunrise or Custom schedules to work in dark mode.

Screen brightness

To suit your taste or the ambient light, you can change the screen's brightness.

1. Select Display from the Settings menu.

2. Tailor Brightness to your liking:

- Adjust the brightness to your liking by dragging the sliders.

- To have your screen's brightness adjusted automatically depending on the surrounding light, use the adaptive brightness button.

Note: Alternatively, you can change the screen's brightness immediately from the Quick Settings window.

Motion smoothness

Raising the screen refresh rate is a simple way to get more realistic animations and smoother scrolling.

1. Go to the Display menu under Settings, and then choose Motion smoothness.
2. Press Apply after touching a choice.

Eye comfort shield

You may find that you sleep better and experience less eye strain as a result of this function. You have the freedom to choose when this feature turns on and off automatically.

1. Press in order to activate this feature from the Settings menu, then go to Display > the Eyes comfort shield.
2. Select the personalization option:
- Adaptive to automatically adjust the color temperature of your screen based on your usage patterns and the current time of day.
- Adjustable to your specific needs, you may program the Eye Comfort Shields to activate at specific times.

- Choose Always on, Sunset-to-sunrise or Custom from the Set schedule menu.

- To adjust the filter's opacity, simply drag the color temperature sliders.

Screen mode

The device comes with a plethora of screen mode options that let you customize the screen quality for different scenarios. Feel free to select the mode that suits you best.

1. Select Display > Screen mode from the Settings menu.

2. To set up another screen mode, touch the option.

- To adjust the white balance, simply drag the slider.

- To change the RGB values by hand, go to the Advance settings.

Font size and font style

You may easily personalize your device by adjusting the font size and style.

o Select Display from the Settings menu. Then, choose the font size and style from the list of possibilities below:

• To choose a different font, just press Font style.

– Press the Download font button to easily add fonts from the Galaxy Store, or touch any font to choose it.

• To see each font with the bold weight, touch Bold fonts.

• Make changes to the font size by dragging the sliders.

Screen zoom

To make the content easier to see, you can adjust the zoom levels.

1. Press Display > Screen zoom in the Settings menu.

2. To adjust the zoom level, simply slide the sliders on your screen.

Full screen application

In the full-screen mode, you may choose which apps to run in the background.

o You may activate this feature and change its settings by going to the Settings, pressing Display, and then tapping Full Screen Applications.

Camera crop

Covering the area around your camera cutout with a black bar is an option.

o To activate this function and configure choices, go to Settings, press Display, then tap on the Camera cutout. From there, tap on applications.

Screen timeout

You can configure the screen to turn off when a certain amount of time has passed.

o Press Display > the Screen timeout in Settings, and then touch a time restriction to set it.

Note: Prolonged viewing of still images (not including Always-On-Display) may result in blurred or even permanently visible afterimages that look like ghosts.

When you're not using the screen, turn it off.

Prevent accidental contact

Keep your screen from detecting touches while your smartphone is in a dark area, such as a pocket or bag.

o To enable the features, go to Settings, press Display, and then choose Accidental touch safeguards.

Touch sensitivity

When you use screen protectors, you can increase your screen's touch sensitivity.

o To enable touch sensitivity, go to Settings and then press Display.

Display charging information

With the screen off, you can see the battery life and how long it will be until the gadget is fully charged.

o Press Display > from the Settings menu, and then Display charging information to turn it on.

Screen saver

Even while the screen is off or charging, it is possible to see pictures or colors.

1. Select Screen saver from the Display menu in the Settings.

2. Please choose an option from the following:

- "None": Hide all screen savers.

- Colors: To access the color-changing screens, tap your choice.

- Picture sheet: Showcase your photographs in a picture table.

- Photo frame Showcase image in a Photo frame.

- Photos: Display photos from your Google Photos account.

3. To see a preview of the screen saver you selected, press the Preview button.

Tip: For more options, touch Settings near the function.

Lift up and wake up

Just raise your device to reveal your screen.

o Press Advanced features, then Motions & gestures, and finally Lift-to-wake in the Settings menu to enable this functionality.

Double click to open screen

Instead of pressing the Side key, you may just double-tap to activate your screen.

o You can activate this function by double-tapping the screen after going to Settings > Advanced features > Motions & gestures.

Double tap to turn off screen

If you prefer not to use the Side key, you can disable the screen by double-tapping.

o Go to the Settings menu, then choose Advanced features, followed by Motions & gestures, and finally This function can be used by double-tapping to turn off your screen.

The screen stays on while watching

You can use front-facing cameras to detect when you're staring at your screen and automatically turn it on.

o Press 🔲 Advanced features in Settings, then touch Motions & gestures. You can activate the feature by touching it, so long as you keep the screen on while looking.

One handed mode

You can change the arrangement of the screen so that you can use just one hand to press your device.

1. To access one-handed mode, go to the Settings menu and select 🔲 Advanced features.

2. Press to enable the function, and then choose one of the following:

• To use this gesture, center your finger on the bottom border of your screen and swipe downward.

• Button: To reduce the screen sizes, press Home twice quickly.

Lock screen and security

By using the screen lock, you may secure your device and safeguard your data.

Screen lock type

You can pick between many types of screens locks that offer medium, high, or no protection at all: swipe, PIN, pattern, password, and none.

Note: A biometric lock can be used to secure your device and any sensitive information stored on it.

Set up a secure screen lock

It is recommended that you secure your device with a passcode, pattern, or PIN. In order to set up and activate the biometric locks, this is required.

1. To secure your displays, go to Settings, and then tap on Lock screen. From there, choose displays lock type and then choose between PIN, Password, or Pattern.

2. To make your lock screen display notifications, press. You can access these choices below:

- Hide content: Prevent alerts from appearing in the Notification window.

- The Notification pane will display any notifications that have been sent.

- Show contents when unlocked: When your screen is not locked, display the contents of your notifications.

- Show notifications: Pick and choose which alerts to show on your Lock screen.

- See alerts right on the Always-On-Display screen by enabling this feature.

3. Hit the Done button to dismiss the menu.

4. Configure the screen lock options:

- The Smart Lock: When trustworthy locations or other devices are detected, your device can be opened automatically. This feature requires the lock of a secure screen.

- Settings for the secure lock: Personalize the settings for the secure lock. This very feature requires the secure displays lock.

- To change the contents and style of your lock screen, simply touch on it.

- Widgets: Use the touch screen to customize the widgets that appear on your lock screen next to the clock.

- If you want to be able to alter the items on your Lock screens, you can do it by holding down on them.

- Always-On-Display: Enable the screen that is always visible.

- The Roaming Clock: Show the time where you are as well as the time at home when you're out and about.

- Concerning the Lock screens: Keep the lock screen software up-to-date.

Chapter Seven
Troubleshooting

You have the option to reset the services on your device and check for software upgrades if needed.

Software updates or system updates

Get the latest software updates for your device and install them. Each service provider has their own set of possibilities.

- o To access the following choices, go to Settings and then click on Software update or System update:

- Keep an eye out for any update: Verify for software updates by hand.

- Make sure there aren't any missing software updates by carefully checking for them.

- Keep updating: Keep going with the interrupted updates.

- A history of software updates: See a list of all the updates that have been installed on your device.

- Using "Smart Updates," your security patches will be installed automatically.

- It's important to keep an eye out for software updates and install them as soon as they become available.

- When the device is connected to a Wi-Fi network, software updates can be downloaded automatically.

- Latest updates: Get details regarding how your current program was installed.

- Software upgrading helpers should be utilized. Software that can be used to install system updates easily.

Reset to default

Clear all network and device settings. Resetting your device to its original settings is another option.

Reset all settings

Except for your security, account, and language settings, resetting your device to factory defaults erases all of your personal data. Private data is unaffected.

1. To reset all of the settings, go to Settings > General management > Reset.

2. Click "Reset settings" and then "Confirm" when asked.

Reset network settings

Reset networks settings allowed me to clear all of my wireless, Bluetooth, and mobile data preferences.

1. To reset the networks settings, go to the Settings menu, and then select General management. Then, hit Reset.

2. Click "Reset settings" and then "Confirm" when asked.

Reset accessibility settings

A reset is available for the device's accessibility settings. There will be no impact on your personal information or the accessibility settings of any apps you download.

1. To reset the accessibility settings, go to the Settings menu, and then select ⚙ General management. Then, hit Reset.

2. Click "Reset settings" and then "Confirm" when asked.

Restore factory data

You can erase all data from the device by resetting it to its factory settings.

Doing this will erase everything from your device, including all of your saved data (photos, movies, music, etc.), as well as your Google and other account settings, app and system data, and the settings of any apps you've downloaded. Nothing happens to the data stored on the external SD card.

Google Devices Protection is activated automatically if you log in to your Google Account on your device and set the lock screen.

Note: It may take up to 24 hours for your re-set Google Account password to take effect across all of your linked devices.

Just before you reset the device:

1. Verify that your desired data has been successfully transferred to your storage facility.

2. Confirm your login credentials by logging into your Google Account.

Regarding device resets:

1. Press ⚙ General management from the Settings menu. Then, touch Reset. Finally, select Factory's data reset.

2. Press the Reset button and follow the on-screen instructions to reset the device.

3. Follow the on-screen instructions to set up your device if it reboots.

www.ingramcontent.com/pod-product-compliance
Lightning Source LLC
LaVergne TN
LVHW051233050326
832903LV00028B/2385

*   9   7   9   8   3   2   7   3   8   6   8   4   6   *